KT-501-510

C153626235

CI53626235

KENT
LIBRARIES & ARCHIVES

weblinks

You don't need a computer to use this book. But, for readers who do have access to the Internet, the book provides links to recommended websites which offer additional information and resources on the subject.

You will find weblinks boxes like this on some pages of the book.

weblinks

For more information about
Tony Hawk, go to
www.waylinks.co.uk
/21CentLives/ExtremeSport

waylinks.co.uk

To help you find the recommended websites easily and quickly, weblinks are provided on our own website, **waylinks.co.uk**. These take you straight to the relevant websites and save you typing in the Internet address yourself.

Internet safety

↗ Never give out personal details, which include: your name, address, school, telephone number, email address, password and mobile number.

↗ Do not respond to messages which make you feel uncomfortable – tell an adult.

↗ Do not arrange to meet in person someone you have met on the Internet.

↗ Never send your picture or anything else to an online friend without a parent's or teacher's permission.

↗ If you see anything that worries you, tell an adult.

A note to adults
Internet use by children should be supervised. We recommend that you install filtering software which blocks unsuitable material.

Website content

The weblinks for this book are checked and updated regularly. However, because of the nature of the Internet, the content of a website may change at any time, or a website may close down without notice. While the Publishers regret any inconvenience this may cause readers, they cannot be responsible for the content of any website other than their own.

WAYLAND

21st CENTURY LIVES
EXTREME SPORTS PEOPLE

Paul Mason

WAYLAND

First published in 2007 by Wayland
Reprinted in 2007

Copyright © Wayland 2007

Editor: Hayley Fairhead
Design: Proof Books

Wayland
338 Euston Road
London NW1 3BH

Wayland
Hachette Children's Books
Level 17/207 Kent Street
Sydney, NSW 2000

All rights reserved.

British Library Cataloguing in Publication Data
Mason, Paul, 1967-
     Extreme sports people. – (21st century lives)
     1. Athletes – Biography – Juvenile literature 2. Extreme
     sports – Juvenile literature
     1. Title
     796'.0922

ISBN 978-0-7502-5045-0

Printed in China

Wayland is a division of Hachette Children's Books,
an Hachette Livre UK Company.

Cover: Tony Hawk performs during his Grand Jam in Orlando,
Florida in 2006.

Picture acknowledgements: Matt Stroshane/Getty Images: front cover
and 11, Marc Le Chelard/AFP/Getty Images: 1 and 14, Francisco
Tremolada: 4, Jorge Visser: 5, Paul Cooper/Rex Features: 6, © Magnolia
Pictures: 7, Jeff Kandas/Getty Images: 8, 9, David Livingston/Getty
Images: 10, Amanda Edwards/Getty Images: 12, Chris Woodage/Buzz
Pictures: 13, Courtesy of Gisela Pulido: 15, Sipa Press/Rex Features: 16,
Getty Images: 17, Rex Features: 18, Agence Zoom/Getty Images: 21, Tim
Aylen/AP/Empics: 19, Vince Bucci/Getty Images: 20.

Contents

WARNING!

All the sports in this book are extremely dangerous.
Never try them without expert instruction and the proper equipment.

Katie Brown
Rock Climber

Katie Brown, one of the world's best young climbers.

" I [enjoy] the atmosphere of being outside climbing, and the feel of the rock. I like how it's a group sport and yet it's also very solitary. There's a lot of freedom about climbing. "

Katie Brown describing what she enjoys about climbing.

Name: Katie Brown

Sport: Rock climbing

Date and place of birth: 30 November 1981, Denver, Colorado

Background: Katie first got into climbing at the age of 12, when she visited an indoor climbing wall. She seems destined to be one of the biggest stars in the world of climbing. She is famous for her 'on-sight', or unrehearsed, climbs of incredibly difficult routes. Katie specializes in 'difficulty climbing': a kind of competition where the competitor who climbs the highest without falling off is the winner.

Major achievements: Katie is best known for her climb of the fiendishly tricky 'Omaha Beach' in Kentucky – at the time, only two (male) climbers had climbed more difficult routes. She has also been U.S. Age Group Champion and World Age Group Champion in rock climbing and she has won several Climbing World Cup contests.

You might not know: Katie says the hardest thing she has ever had to do is make a speech: "I'm not a super-talkative person," she says.

Become a pro: Katie has always been determined not to make any excuses for herself. She says: "in the climbing community it's a big thing to make excuses. Saying stuff like, 'I can't do that route because I'm too tall' or 'I couldn't reach that hold because I'm too short.' I try not to use those excuses. Sometimes size is a factor, but usually there are ways around it."

Katie originally came from Denver, Colorado, a city right by the Rocky Mountains. This sounds like a great place to learn to climb – but Katie didn't start climbing until her family moved from Denver to Kentucky, when she was 12!

Soon after she reached Kentucky, Katie started climbing on an artificial wall. These have holds bolted to them, to give climbers a chance to practise different moves. Katie's teachers soon saw how talented she was. They encouraged her to climb using combinations of holds that were more and more difficult.

Soon Katie was climbing outdoors on real rock. This is more dangerous than indoor climbing. Holds can break off, and equipment is more likely to fail. The climbers go higher, so if they fall, the landings are much harder and injuries are more likely.

Katie's best-known climb is 'Omaha Beach' in Kentucky. She climbed this when she was just 17. 'Omaha Beach' is named after a battle that took place during the Second World War. U.S. soldiers were trapped on the beach by enemy fire. 'Omaha Beach', the climb, has a spot where climbers also get trapped. Getting out of this tricky spot is the most difficult move on the climb – climbers call this the 'crux' move.

Katie normally likes to climb smoothly, but there was no smooth route over the 'crux' move on 'Omaha Beach'. Instead she had to 'dyno' – leap powerfully upwards to grab a hold, then pull herself up. After this, the rest of the climb went well. Katie found out when she finished the climb that it was graded 5.13d – making it the hardest grade ever climbed by a female climber without practising the moves! At the time, the world's hardest climbing route was graded 5.14.

Katie has since moved back to Denver. She has begun to climb some of the difficult rock routes nearby, as well as travelling to Europe for competitions and to climb new routes there. As her climbing continues to improve, she carries on climbing increasingly tricky routes.

Katie tackling a tough, overhanging route at Aromas de Montgroni, Spain.

"She's a very strong on-sight climber, with a very smooth and deliberate style. I look forward to seeing what she does in the future..."

Pioneering female rock climber Lynn Hill.

weblinks

For more information about Katie Brown, go to
www.waylinks.co.uk/21CentLives/ExtremeSports

David Belle
Traceur

David Belle, inventor of parkour.

Name: David Belle

Sport: *Parkour*/free running

Date and place of birth: 29 April 1973, Fécamp, France

Background: David is one of the most famous *traceurs* (*traceur* means 'one who goes fast') in the world. *Traceurs* are people who take part in the sport of *parkour*.

Inspired by his father's and grandfather's stories of heroic rescues by firemen, David began to train in gymnastics, athletics, climbing and martial arts. At 15, he began to fuse all these activites together into a new sport, named *parkour*.

Teams played for: One of the original members of the *Yamakasi parkour* group. The group split up after disagreeing over a 2001 film about them, called *Yamakasi*. Since then, David has run his own training school for *traceurs*, as well as taking part in TV and movie work.

Major achievements: David invented a whole new sport called *parkour*, which some people know as 'free running'. He has since performed *parkour* stunts for advertisements and films.

Become a pro: David teaches *parkour*, and says it is important to be hard on yourself in training. He says: "My personal philosophy is: train yourself while crying, and you will win while laughing."

❝ Don't be in a hurry. Take the time to build yourself, and get in good physical condition… First, do it. Second, do it well. Third, do it well and fast. ❞

David Belle giving advice to people who would like to learn *parkour*.

David Belle in a chase sequence from one of his movies Banlieue 13.

David originally came from a small town on the coast of northern France. His grandfather had been a fireman, and his father had been a soldier, then a fireman. David grew up hearing stories about the bravery and skill of firemen in making rescues from tall, burning buildings.

David was sports-mad, and became good at athletics, climbing, gymnastics and martial arts. He left school at 15 years old so that he could spend more time taking part in sports.

Inspired by the heroic firefighting stories he had heard as a child, David would often imagine situations where he could use his sports skills in real-life situations. How would he be able to get to fire victims in order to rescue them? How would he escape from burning buildings without using the stairs?

David began to practice running, vaulting, leaping, climbing and balancing. He trained himself to be able to move quickly through, around and sometimes over buildings.

When he was still 15, David moved to Lisses, in the city of Paris. Here, he met other people who were interested in the same skills. They formed a group called *Yamakasi*, which means 'high energy' when used in French. The *Yamakasi* worked out the best ways to scale high walls, leap from buildings and use their energy to take unusual routes through the city. They would run along the tops of walls, leap over obstacles and jump from high places. The sport of *parkour* had been born. The people who took part became known as *traceurs*.

David worked as a fireman, like his grandfather, father and older brother, and joined the French army. But the lure of *parkour* was too strong! David left to become a full-time *traceur*. Since then, he has performed *parkour* in advertisements for the BBC, Nike and Nissan, as well as several feature films. His latest was *Banlieue 13*, which was released with the English title *District B13*, in 2006. The film quickly entered the top 10 movies list.

"One of the main points of the philosophy behind *parkour* is being able to help people... To teach them the way themselves, to gain confidence in themselves, building up from simple moves to more complex things, to teach them that they are worthwhile people."

Chris Hayes-Kossmann, fellow *traceur*.

weblinks

For more information about David Belle, go to
www.waylinks.co.uk/21CentLives/ExtremeSports

Ricky Carmichael
Motocross Racer

Ricky Carmichael is a champion in one of the most dangerous sports – off-road motorbike racing.

" I'm doing something I love to do... I don't know what to say, except the wins keep coming. I've had a great career and I'll try to get as many more [wins] as I can. "

Ricky Carmichael

Name: Ricky Carmichael

Sport: Motocross and supercross

Nicknames: RC and the GOAT (which stands for 'Greatest Of All Time').

Date and place of birth: 27 November 1979, Clearwater, Florida, USA

Background: Ricky is famous as the world's best-ever outdoor motocross racer.

Major achievements: The AMA Motocross Championship is the hardest off-road motorcycling competition in the world. Ricky has been the AMA Motocross Champion a record seven times, and has won over 100 professional races.

Ricky also races supercross, an indoor version of motocross. He was AMA Supercross champion five times by the end of the 2006 season.

Teams played for: Ricky finished his motorcycle career racing for Suzuki. When he retired from full-time racing in 2006, rumours suggested that Ricky might start racing on four wheels, in the US NASCAR car racing championship.

You might not know: Ricky became the highest-paid motocross rider ever, with a salary of $2 million a year!

Become a pro: Ricky's first season in top-flight racing was not a success, with bad results and injuries. He was not put off, and his determination to succeed helped him go on to become the most successful racer ever.

Motocross and supercross are sports where riders on special motorbikes race each other around a course of bumps, jumps and turns. The riders sometimes do huge jumps, high into the air. Motocross races usually take place outdoors on a course of mixed natural and artificial obstacles. Supercross races normally take place in giant baseball or American football stadiums, on artificial courses.

As you can guess, the huge jumps and high speeds mean that motocross and supercross are very dangerous. Riders who crash during a race can be badly injured. The most successful racer ever is Ricky Carmichael.

Ricky first started riding a motorbike at 3 years old. Other American kids spent their weekends playing baseball or football. Not Ricky! He was out racing motocross. Ricky broke all amateur records for race wins, and by 1996 he was ready to turn professional in the very last race of the season.

Motocross races are divided up according to how big the engine of the bike is. Ricky spent his first two seasons in the 125cc category. He won the national championship both years, and by 1999 was ready to move to the 250cc category. Ricky had a tricky first season. He kept crashing, and injured himself early on. Injuries – especially broken bones – are common in motocross. Many riders have bones they once broke, which are held together by metal pins and plates. Ricky's injuries and crashes meant he didn't win a single race in the 250cc category until 2000.

Once Ricky did start winning though, he couldn't stop. He races in two main categories: the first – his best – is 250cc motocross, his second is supercross. He won the national motocross title in 2000, 2001, 2002, 2003, 2004, 2005 and 2006. In 2002, Ricky recorded the first ever 'perfect season' – he won every single race. 2002 was a good year for Ricky – he also got married to his girlfriend Ursula. They now live together in Florida. The 'perfect season' had previously seemed impossible, but Ricky managed it again in 2004!

Ricky also races supercross. He won the national supercross title in 2001, 2002, 2003, 2005 and 2006. Ricky missed the 2004 supercross season, because he had to have surgery on a knee injury he had suffered the previous year.

Ricky at the Steel City raceway in Pennsylvannia on his way to the perfect season in 2004.

By 2006 – which he hinted would be his last year racing – Ricky had won well over 100 races as a professional. He had become the greatest motocross rider of all time.

"They don't call him the GOAT [Greatest Of All Time] for nothing. I'm working my hardest to be able to run with him. Sometimes I get frustrated because I'm riding my best and I still have a long way to go."

Ricky's rival Chad Reed during the 2006 motocross season.

weblinks

For more information about Ricky Carmichael, go to

www.waylinks.co.uk/21CentLives/ExtremeSports

Tony Hawk
Skateboarder

Tony Hawk, the world's most famous skater.

> " I'm pretty happy with the way things turned out. I mean, I never thought [at the beginning] that I could make a career out of skateboarding. "
>
> Tony Hawk

Name: Tony Hawk

Sport: Skateboarding

Nickname: 'Birdman'

Date and place of birth: 12 May 1968, San Diego, California, USA

Background: Tony is recognized as the best vert-ramp skater in the world. (A vert ramp is a steep skateboarding ramp with vertical sections at each end.)

Teams played for: Tony started on the Dogtown skate team at 12 years old, and later rode for Stacey Peralta's Bones Brigade skate team.

Major achievements: Tony invented many of the toughest tricks in modern skateboarding. His most famous is the '900' – a jump in which he spins through the air two-and-a-half times before landing.

In competition, Tony has won (among other things): 1982 Rusty Harris series final competition; 1983 Del Mar Spring Nationals (California); 1984 NSA-Del Mar Skatepark; 1986 Transworld Skateboarding Championships; 2002 X-Games vert doubles (with Andy Macdonald).

You might not know: Tony is said to be a descendant of the English explorer Henry Hudson, the man believed to have discovered the Hudson River on the USA's East Coast.

Become a pro: Tony has never been satisfied with his own performances, and always tries to improve his skating – even when he wins!

Crowds wait to be wowed by one of Tony's trademark tricks.

Tony Hawk now admits that he was a trial to his parents. "I was the terrible youth," he says. "I was a hyper, rail-thin geek" (he was full of energy, skinny and a geek!). Tony's energy finally began to find a use when his brother gave him his first skateboard. Tony was aged nine, and he has been skating ever since.

Tony took skating very seriously. If he entered a contest and didn't do as well as he'd hoped, Tony would go into a sulk – he would sulk even if he'd won! He would go up to his room and sit quietly with his cat, Zorro.

Three years after first picking up a skateboard, at just 12 years old, Tony was part of the famous Dogtown skate team, which contained many of California's best skaters. At 14, he turned professional, and by the age of 16 he was being called the best skater in the world. By the time he was 17, Tony had earned enough to buy his own house and was touring the world for skating events – even though most of his friends were still at school!

Suddenly, skateboarding lost popularity. The market for skateboards and skating gear almost disappeared. The money for sponsored riders dried up, and Tony found it hard to make a living.

During the mid 1990s, skateboarding became increasingly popular once more. Tony's skateboard and clothing companies (Birdhouse Skateboards and Hawk Clothing) became more successful. Then, in 1999, Tony designed the computer game 'Tony Hawk's Pro Skater'. The game has been a bestseller ever since.

Tony has appeared in lots of TV shows, including *The Simpsons* and *Sex and the City*. His movie appearances include the documentary *Dogtown and Z-Boys*, which many people think is the best skating movie ever made.

Tony no longer takes part in contests, but he still skates most days. He regularly appears in skating events around the world. The audiences are full of people who have come to see the world's greatest vert-ramp skateboarder.

> "The kids were so excited to get money from Tony Hawk, they didn't want to cash the check (sic), but we decided we'd better. Tony hand-wrote some suggestions on the skatepark plan, and we were all sure that we should be the one to keep [the skatepark plan]."
>
> Recipient of a Tony Hawk Foundation award to build a new skatepark.

weblinks

For more information about Tony Hawk, go to
www.waylinks.co.uk/21CentLives/ExtremeSports

Mat Hoffman
BMX Rider

Mat Hoffman, the world's most famous BMX rider.

> **If you want to experience all of the successes and pleasure in life, you have to be willing to accept all the pain and failure that comes with it. I don't let fear hold myself [sic] back from living life.**
>
> Mat Hoffman

Name: Mat Hoffman

Sport: BMX riding

Nickname: 'The Condor'

Date and place of birth: 9 January, 1972, Edmond, Oklahoma, USA

Background: The youngest pro rider in BMX history, Mat invented many of BMX riding's most famous and most difficult tricks. Today, he is known as the best BMX rider in the world. He holds the world record for the highest jump ever made on a bicycle: it was over 15 metres high.

Major achievements: Mat was the first BMX rider ever to land a '900' (two-and-a-half spins in the air) in competition.

In 2002, he performed a 'no-hands 900': the same trick but taking your hands off the handlebars. No one has ever repeated this spectacular move.

You might not know: Mat once jumped his bike off a 1-kilometre-high cliff in Norway – before opening his parachute and gliding to earth!

Mat has appeared in the Vin Diesel movie *Triple X*, performing bike stunts, and in *Jackass – The Movie*, among other shows.

Become a pro: Mat is famous for his toughness – he once had an operation to repair his damaged knee without a pain-killing injection!

Mat Hoffman is the most successful BMX rider ever. His speciality is 'freestyle BMX': riding a BMX bike on a vert ramp (the same as the ones skateboarders use: a steep ramp with vertical sections at each end). Like skaters, freestyle BMX riders use their speed to do amazing jumps from the top of each side of the ramp.

Mat first began competing at the age of 13. Just three years later, he had turned professional. He was the youngest pro-rider the BMX world had ever seen – before he'd even finished school! Mat quickly became the biggest star on the BMX scene.

In 1991, when Mat was 19 years old, he decided to split up with his sponsor and form Hoffman Promotions, his own company. Mat also decided to try and build the best BMX bike in the world. The bikes Mat had been riding kept breaking, so the 'best' bike had to be strong enough not to break, but still light enough for performing tricks. Mat ended up forming Hoffman Bikes, his second company. He was still only 20 years old!

Mat has always been known for his ability to invent new tricks that will wow the judges in contests. He invented some of the most radical tricks ever done on a BMX bike. They include:
• The first-ever competition '900' and 'no-hands 900'.
• The 'flip-fakie', in which the bike and rider do a backflip together, before landing backwards!
• The 'flair', a backflip with a 180° spin.

Mat carried on entering – and usually winning – BMX contests. But he also wanted to help the sport of BMX develop. He came up with the 'Bicycle Stunt' events, where top riders could demonstrate their tricks to huge crowds all across the U.S.A. The events were so popular that in 1995 they began to be shown on T.V.

Next, Mat formed the Hoffman Sports Association, which organizes BMX events around the world. In 2005, he was elected President of the International BMX Freestyle Federation. At 33, Mat had managed to fit a lot into a short time. What did he have to say about it? "I feel like I'm just getting started!"

A 'no-hands 900', 5 metres above the top of the ramp.

"What's left to say about a guy who ignored all established limits and redefined vert riding – at age 15?"

Ride, magazine article.

weblinks

For more information about Mat Hoffman, go to
www.waylinks.co.uk/21CentLives/ExtremeSports

Gisela Pulido
Kitesurfer

Gisela Pulido, who first became the world's best female kitesurfer at the age of ten.

❝ After breakfast I head out to school, and then I have to first watch my most favourite [TV show], *The Simpsons*. Then I go kiting, swimming, stretching, watch some more TV and if there is really nothing else to do, I enjoy going and playing with my friends or a PlayStation game. ❞

Gisela describes a typical day.

Name: Gisela Pulido

Sport: Kitesurfing

Date and place of birth: 14 January 1994, Barcelona, Spain

Background: Gisela started bodyboarding when she was just three years old. She could snowboard and skateboard by the time she was five.

She has since become the youngest kitesurfing world champion ever. By 2005, Gisela had already won the title twice at the ages of ten and eleven years old!

Sponsors: Gisela is sponsored by the surf companies Rip Curl and Da Kine, and kite company Airush.

Major achievements: She became World Kitesurfing Champion in 2004 and 2005.

You might not know: Gisela dreams of becoming a vet, because she says she "loves animals".

Become a pro: Gisela says that part of her success is because she enjoys kitesurfing so much. When asked about her plans for the future, she said: "Stay at the best level, do new tricks, but above all continue to have fun!".

Gisela's ability to work out new tricks in the air is one of the main reasons she has been so successful.

Kitesurfing's biggest star is Gisela Pulido. Gisela first became the world kitesurfing champion in 2004. Amazingly, she was just ten years old!

Gisela was born in Barcelona, Spain. She has always been sports-mad, and started bodyboarding on the city's beaches when she was just three. By the time she was five, Gisela could snowboard and skateboard as well.

Around this time, Gisela's father took up kitesurfing. She dreamed of trying the sport, and making the huge jumps and spins in the air she saw the kitesurfers performing. But Gisela was too small! She needed to weigh at least 35kg to be allowed to use kitesurfing equipment.

Finally, in 2000, Gisela passed the 35kg barrier and was able to try kitesurfing. She quickly became an expert. To help Gisela's kitesurfing get even better, her family moved from Barcelona to Tarifa, on Spain's southern coast. Tarifa is famous for its windy conditions. Windsurfers and kitesurfers come from all round the world to sail there.

Gisela also started at a different school, which finished at 2 p.m. This was a big change from before, when she had finished at 5 p.m. The change meant that Gisela was able to train much harder than before. As she says: "Now that I'm in Tarifa, and finish school at 2 p.m. every day, I

have a lot of spare time to train in the hard conditions." All the training began to pay off in 2004, when Gisela was ten. She won the Kitesurfing World Championships for the first time. This was despite most of the other competitors being between two and three times her age! She carried on her great success in 2005. Gisela won five of the six contests for the world's top kitesurfers. To cap it all, she again won the World Championship at the end of the year.

Gisela's dreams for the future include the hope that kitesurfing might one day be an Olympic sport. If it does, she will be hoping to win an Olympic kitesurfing gold, to go with her World Championship trophies!

"She only rides for fun, and she is always happy when she is riding. Competing is no pressure for her or us, and for Gisela it's all about having as much fun as she can have during her school holidays."

Gisela's father

weblinks

For more information about Gisela Pulido, go to
www.waylinks.co.uk/21CentLives/ExtremeSports

Kelly Slater

Surfer

Kelly Slater, one of the most successful surfers of all time.

> " I was probably at [the] beach 12 hours a day. It was sort of the scene when I was a little kid. "

Kelly explaining one of the reasons he became such a good surfer when he was so young.

Name: Kelly Slater

Sport: Surfing

Nickname: 'Jimmy' (because of his role as Jimmy Slade in the hit TV show *Baywatch*)

Date and place of birth: 11 February 1972, Cocoa Beach, Florida, USA

Background: Kelly is the most successful competitive surfer of all time. So famous that he got a big shout from Queen Latifah at the MTV Awards in 2003, Kelly has spread the popularity of surfing around the world.

Major achievements: Kelly has been the world surfing champion eight times, winning in 1992, 1994, 1995, 1996, 1997, 1998, 2005 and 2006.

As well as the year-long World Championship competition, Kelly has won several one-off events. The most famous of these is the Quiksilver in Memorial of Eddie Aikau Big-Wave Contest, in 2002. In May 2005, Kelly became the first surfer ever to score 20 out of 20 in a competition.

You might not know: Kelly has been a model for the Versace fashion company.

Become a pro: Kelly is famous for being very competitive and very dedicated. He is often in the water practising longer than anyone else.

Kelly Slater is sometimes called 'the Michael Jordan of Surfing' (Michael Jordan is the world's most famous basketball player). He has helped to make surfing one of the coolest extreme sports around. There has been an explosion in the number of people surfing since Kelly became famous.

Kelly spent his childhood near the beach in Florida, USA. He learnt to surf at the Third Street North Beach, and spent most of his free time there with his brothers Sean and Stephen. The three boys spent so much time at the beach that their mother decided to get a job at The Islander Hut. The Hut was a nearby snack bar, so she could keep an eye on them more easily!

Kelly pulls into a tube at Pipeline in Hawaii. His tuberiding at Pipeline has helped Kelly win the world title several times.

Soon, Kelly's talent had started to attract attention. By the time he was 8, the local surf shop had had a board specially made for Kelly. That same year, he won his first ever contest. Everything was not perfect, though: Kelly's parents' marriage was breaking up, and his father left their home in 1983.

Kelly carried on entering and winning big surf contests. He finally turned professional in November 1990. Kelly soon began to make his mark in the biggest contests, winning his first world title in 1992. He would go on to win 7 more world titles. Kelly stopped competing full-time in 1999, at the age of 27, but came back to surfing to win further world titles in 2005 and 2006.

As well as surfing, in 1992 and 1993 Kelly acted in the TV show *Baywatch*. At the time this was the most-watched show in the world. Kelly played lifeguard and surfer Jimmy Slade. It was years before Australian surfers stopped calling him 'Jimmy' instead of Kelly!

While acting on *Baywatch*, Kelly met Pamela Anderson, who later became his girlfriend for a while. He has had several other glamorous girlfriends, including the supermodel Giselle.

As well as surfing, Kelly works to help several charities. One of these is Reef Check, a group that works to preserve coral reefs around the world. Another charity he supports is the Make-A-Wish Foundation, which helps children with life-threatening injuries or diseases. Kelly also supports the Kelly Slater Scholarship Fund at his old high school, which helps students from single-parent families.

"When he stays at a motel and he puts his trash out, people will come by digging through it to see what he ate, like they're looking for some kind of candy bar wrapper that makes him superhuman. But to us, he's just Kelly."

Kelly's long-time friend Matt Kechele

weblinks

For more information about Kelly Slater, go to
www.waylinks.co.uk/21CentLives/ExtremeSports

Tanya Streeter
Freediver

Tanya Streeter spends time practising in the swimming pool.

> **❝ My respect for the ocean borders on fear. I'm comfortable underwater, but never too comfortable. Often times I'm miles and miles offshore, with nothing but a rope and a few friends. You really gain a deep respect for what's out there. ❞**
>
> **Tanya Streeter**

Name: Tanya Streeter

Sport: Freediving

Date and place of birth: 10 January, 1973, Cayman Islands

Background: Tanya spent a lot of time swimming and diving with friends when she was younger. She could often be found on the beach near her home in the Caribbean.

Tanya is now one of the most successful freedivers in the world. Freediving involves holding your breath as you dive as deep underwater as possible.

Major achievements: In 2002, she became the World No-limits record holder by diving down 160 metres in one breath. In 2003, she was World Variable Ballast record holder.

You might not know: Tanya can hold her breath underwater for 6 minutes and 8 seconds!

Become a pro: Tanya trains very hard for her record-breaking dives, but she says that they are always a team effort. After one dive, she wrote that: "I believed I could do it because they [the team] believed I could do it."

Tanya descends on a sled for one of her record breaking dives.

all dive down looking for interesting shells. "I've been in the water all my life," she says. Even then, though, she was competing with the other divers: "I guess I always dived a little deeper than the other kids".

Tanya's family originally came from England, and she left Grand Cayman to study in Brighton, on the south coast. After finishing school and university Tanya soon headed back to the Caribbean and, once again, began to spend her free time on the beach or in the ocean.

In 1997, Tanya went on a freediving course. By the end of the day she had managed to dive to 29 metres. Her instructors were amazed, and immediately offered to coach her. Tanya took her training seriously: she runs or goes to the gym every day, and trains in the pool five times a week. Within just a few months she had begun setting world records.

Deep underwater, there is so much weight of water pressing on your body that it has strange effects. During the deepest dives, Tanya begins to feel light-headed and her legs become partly paralyzed. Her lungs are crushed down to the size of a clenched fist. She cannot wear a mask, and the pressure causes her eyeballs to change shape, so her vision blurs. Way down deep, Tanya's heart beats at just 15 beats a minute. (Most humans average about 80 beats per minute!)

Despite the amazing challenges involved, Tanya has set world records for many different types of freediving. These include several overall world records (for both men and women). Tanya once held overall world records in three of the different freediving categories, making her the world's most successful freediver.

Tanya Streeter has become world-famous for her record-setting activities in the sport of freediving. Freediving is highly dangerous – it involves diving as deep as possible while holding your breath. In 2002, Tanya set an incredible world record by diving down 160 metres on one breath. If that doesn't sound much, think of it this way: it's the same distance as 29 giraffes standing on one another's heads!

Tanya was born on the Caribbean island of Grand Cayman. She and her friends would often go swimming after school or at the weekend. They would

"Tanya has a rare composure and grace. She's uniquely attuned to being in the underwater world."

Tec Clark, captain of the US freediving team.

weblinks

For more information about Tanya Streeter, go to
www.waylinks.co.uk/21CentLives/ExtremeSports

Shaun White

Snowboarder

Shaun White collects his 'Best US Olympian' and 'Best Male Action Athlete' awards at the 2006 ESPY Awards.

> **"** It's fun to ride at contests and stuff, but I have the most fun snowboarding when it's just me and my brother... I get so comfortable when I'm with people I like to ride with that I just start learning tricks... I think it's so much fun when snowboarding's like that. **"**
>
> **Shaun White**

Name: Shaun White

Sport: Snowboarding and skateboarding

Nickname: 'The Flying Tomato': because of his bright-red hair!

Date and place of birth: 3 September 1986, Carlsbad, California, USA

Background: The hottest star on the snowboard scene and gold medalist at the 2006 Winter Olympics, Shaun is also a top-level skateboarder.

Teams played for: Shaun's main sponsors are Burton Snowboards and Birdhouse Skateboards.

Major achievements: He became the 2006 Winter Olympic gold medalist in the half-pipe; winner of 6 gold and 2 silver snowboard medals at the X-Games (the world's biggest extreme sports competition) and winner of 1 silver skateboard medal at the X-Games.

You might not know: Shaun was the first person to compete in the winter and summer X-Games at 2 different sports (snowboarding and skateboarding).

Become a pro: Try lots of different sports, you might be good at more than one! Shaun is famous for practising a range of different board sports. As well as snowboarding and skateboarding, he's also a mean surfer!

Shaun in the Snowboard Halfpipe Final, at the 2006 Winter Olympic Games.

try snowboarding. In the end, his father was forced to have snowboarding lessons – so that he could teach Shaun how to do it!

Shaun was so fearless that he went really fast on a snowboard. His mother tried to think of a way to slow him down. In the end she told Shaun he could only go snowboarding if he rode backwards! Riding backwards, or 'fakie', is a key skill in snowboarding. Shaun probably didn't think so at the time, but his mum was doing him a big favour!

A few months after starting to snowboard, Shaun also began skateboarding. When he was nine, Shaun met top skater Tony Hawk (see pages 10-11) on a snowboard trip. Tony's company, Birdhouse Skateboards, was one of Shaun's sponsors when he became a professional skater at the age of 16.

Shaun became a professional snowboarder when he was just 13. He was already seen as a future star – his nickname back then was 'Future Boy'. Shaun became known for linking together huge jumps very smoothly, in a way no one had seen before. He quickly became the one to beat in any snowboard competition, and it was no surprise when he won Olympic gold at the age of 20, in 2006.

Very few people are talented enough to reach the top in an extreme sport. Shaun White has reached the highest level in two extreme sports – snowboarding and skateboarding!

Shaun has not always been the fit superstar of today. When he was a small boy he had problems with his heart .By the time Shaun was five, he had already had two operations on his heart. Fortunately Shaun recovered from his health problems.

When he was six, Shaun went on a family trip to the mountains in California. His brother, Jesse, had a go at snowboarding. Shaun wanted to try it too, but was told he was too young for lessons. Shaun was desperate to

> "Shaun is capable of doing anything on a snowboard or a skateboard. He has always had the motivation and the talent, but he now has the strength and confidence to push the perceived limits of what is considered possible."
>
> Tony Hawk

weblinks

For more information about Shaun White, go to

www.waylinks.co.uk/21CentLives/ExtremeSports

Other Extreme Sports Stars

Jon Jon Florence, Hawaii, USA – Surfer

Jon Jon was born 18 October 1992, but he is already the hottest property in surfing. He is a poor kid who grew up on the beach in Hawaii, and turned surfing talent into big-money sponsorship deals before he was even a teenager. Jon Jon has been 4 times US National Junior Champion, and 8 times winner of Hawaii's Rell Sunn Menehune Championship (which he first won at 5 years old).

Jon Jon's greatest achievement so far is to be the youngest surfer ever to compete in the Triple Crown surfing event. The Triple Crown is one of the toughest surf contests in the world. The reason is the size, power and difficulty of the waves.

In 2005, the waves for the contest were huge. Jon Jon, who was 13 years old and not yet 5 feet tall, won his first-round contest surfing in waves more than twice his own height. By the afternoon, the waves had got bigger, reaching 4.4 metres. "That's probably the biggest Haleiwa [the name of the surf spot where the contest took place] I've ever surfed," said Jon Jon. "It was really hard… Every time I tried to do a turn the tail of my board just slid out. It was exciting… but it was pretty scary." He was knocked out in the second round – but most people think that once he's grown a little, Jon Jon is sure to be winning big contests like this one.

Aaron Hadlow, UK – Kitesurfer

At an age when most kids are just thinking about what they might do when they leave school, Aaron was already World Kitesurfing Champion. He first won the title at 16, having only been kitesurfing for 4 years. He has since become World Champion another two times.

Aaron got into kitesurfing on a family holiday to Cabarete, in the Dominican Republic. He picked up his first sponsor at just 13 years old. Today, Aaron is famous for performing new moves in competitions, and says that, "in the future I hope to carry on and become the Kelly Slater (see pages 16-17) of kitesurfing". And the best thing about being world champion? "The lifestyle, that's the best thing by far," says Aaron, "being able to travel the world doing the sport you love, and meeting and seeing so many new people and places."

Brian Lopes, USA – Cyclist

Brian Lopes is one of the greatest extreme-sports cyclists ever. He learned to ride a bike at the age of 4, raced BMX as an amateur all through his childhood, and turned professional at the age of 17. Brian then moved on to mountain biking, where he has won over 17 titles, including 5 World Cup contests and 3 world championships.

Brian's speciality events are downhill, 4x and duel mountain biking. Downhill racers go as fast as possible down a pre-designed course, one after the other: the fastest wins. 4x and duel are races between 4 or 2 competitors, with the fastest going through to the next round. All three events require speed, courage and great bike-handling skills.

Tracey Mosley, UK – Mountain biker

Tracey specializes in the heart-stopping sport of downhill mountain biking, and is one of the world's best racers. Downhill mountain bikers plunge down steep, rocky, tree-lined courses one after another. The racer with the fastest time wins.

By 2006, after 4 years at the top of her sport, Tracey was number 1 in the world rankings, but she still had big plans for the future. When asked what she hoped to achieve in the rest of the year, Tracey said: "I want to win the [downhill biking] World Cup. I got second [place] last year, my closest yet, so I'm hoping I can do better this year. Also, I'm going to aim for the World Champs. Usually I view it as just another race on the circuit… but I want to change that and make it a real focus for me this year."

Sofia Mulanovich, Peru – Surfer

Peruvian surfer Sofia Mulanovich is used to breaking records. She was the first (and so far, only) Peruvian surfer to win a World Championship Tour (WCT) event. Sofia topped that when she was the overall winner of the WCT in 2004, becoming world champion – and the first South American ever to win the biggest prize in surfing!

Sofia learnt to swim at three years old, and was boogie-boarding by the time she was five. At nine, she switched to standing up on a surfboard, and by the age of 12 Sofia was travelling to international contests. She won the 2004 World Surfing Championship at the age of 21. Sofia lost her title in 2005. She was beaten by her friend Chelsea Georgeson of Australia. It was a close contest though, with the world title only decided at the very last contest of the year.

Dani Pedrosa, Spain – Motorcyclist

Dani Pedrosa got his first motorbike at the age of four. It had stabilizer wheels on the side, so that it couldn't topple over! Dani didn't have long to wait before getting a 'proper' motorbike, though. It arrived when he was six years old, and was used for racing against friends in the small Spanish village of *Castellar del Valles*, where he lived.

Dani began taking part in serious competition at the age of 11, when he raced in the Spanish Minibikes series, coming second overall. From then on he hasn't looked back.

Today, Dani is a hotshot motorcycle racer. He was the youngest-ever world champion in the 125cc division (in 2003, at the age of 18) and the 250cc division (in 2004, at 19). He won the 250cc division again in 2005. In 2006, Dani moved into the MotoGP class, where riders race on 990cc bikes at speeds of over 200mph. He won his first race in Shanghai in March 2006. Dani seems guaranteed to be one of motorcycling's stars of the future.

Lesley McKenna, Britain – Snowboarder

Lesley McKenna is Britain's top snowboarder – even though she was 21 before she learnt to slide! Originally from Scotland, Lesley now spends much of each year on the road, taking part in snowboarding contests around the world. Lesley took part in the half-pipe contests in the 2002 and 2006 Winter Olympics, and has been competing in the Snowboard World Cup since 1998. Her best contest results have been two World Cup wins.

Lesley is well known for her out-of-competition riding, which has often featured in snowboard movies, and she spent a large part of the 2007 season filming for the *Last Winter* movie project. One of Lesley's aims in these movies is to inspire other young women to take up snowboarding. She says: "It's the most amazing sport in the world, is done in some of the most beautiful places and by some of the nicest people I have met."

Index

21st Century Lives

Contents of all books in the series:

WAYLAND